Little Red Riding Hood

Phonics Consultant: Susan Purcell

Illustrator: Monika Filipina

Concept: Fran Bromage

Miles Kelly

As you read aloud, focus on the r sound (as in red)

Once upon a time, there was a little girl who wore a red skirt, red shoes and a red hood. Her name was Little Red Riding Hood.

Say the words as you spot things beginning with r.

2 **Stick on** their stickers.

red

rabbit

roof

One day her mother said, "Grandma is really not well. Can you run round to see her right away?"

What a good try! Put a gold star here. Well done!

Use your stickers to **spell** some words with the r sound.

rat   rice   ring   room

Emphasize
the w sound
(as in wood)

Red Riding Hood walked through the wood to Grandma's house. A wolf was waiting for her to wander closer – then he jumped out!

Sound out these words with the w sound.

way   win   wig   wool

well   wasp   web

"Well, hello," growled the wolf,
"do you want to play?"

"No, thank you. I'm walking
to Grandma's house,"
said Red Riding Hood,
looking worried.

Well
done!

Use your stickers to **spell** more words beginning with w.

week   wash   worm   Window

"Before you leave the wood,
why not pick some flowers?"
said the wolf.
"I should! What a good idea,"
said Red Riding Hood.

Use your stickers to **spell** some words with the oo sound.

would   **could**   **foo**t   **look**

"What a treasure you are!" said the wolf. "It's a pleasure to meet you," and off he ran.

Well done!

Sound out these words, which all use the **zh** sound.

measure   leisure   television
casual   usual

But that naughty wolf was soon knocking at Grandma's door. Grandma knew it was not Red Riding Hood, so she hid in the wardrobe.

Sound out these words with the n sound in different positions.

neck　　noon　　knot　　gnaw

funny　　line　　pan　　corn

When the wolf walked in, Grandma was nowhere to be seen. He put on her nightgown and nightcap.

Well done!

Use your stickers to **spell** some words beginning with the n sound.

nest   knit   knee   gnome

As the wolf got into bed, Red Riding Hood knocked on the door.

Straight away she saw something wasn't right.

Use your arrow stickers to **point** to things that rhyme with s**aw**.

Sound out these words, which all use the or sound.

sort   born   horse

jaw   straw   autumn

"Poor Grandma!"
she said, your face
looks very odd!"

Well done!

Use your stickers to **spell** some more words with the **or** sound.

f o r k   sh o r t   y a w n   s a u cer

Emphasize
the ear sound
(as in dear)

"Hello, my dear,"
said the wolf.
"Do not fear.
Come and sit
near me!"

Use your stickers to **complete** these sentences with the ear sound.

"What big ears you have, Grandma!"
"All the better to hear you with."

12

"My, what big **eyes** you have, Grandma," said Red Riding Hood.

"All the better to see you with," replied the sly wolf.

Well done!

Sound out these words with the ie sound.

cry   fly   dry   tie   pie

ride   time   high   night

13

Highlight the ee sound (as in teeth)

"And your teeth are huge!" gasped Little Red Riding Hood.

"All the better to eat you with!" said the wolf, jumping to his feet.

Red Riding Hood screamed!

Sound out these words with the ee sound.

need   geese   tree   sweet

bead   treat   steam

The wolf threw off the nightdress and Red Riding Hood ran away as fast as she could, fearing for her life.

Well done!

Say the words as you spot things with the f sound.

Stick on their stickers.

face

fingers

wolf

 15

A woodcutter heard Red Riding Hood screaming. He rushed in holding his axe.

"I'll have that wolf's tail!" he hollered.

Say the names of the things with the h sound, as you spot them.

hood   hand   head

hedge   handle

But the big grey wolf escaped with his tail. He ran away and never came near Red Riding Hood again – hooray!

Well done!

Use your stickers to **spell** some words with the ai sound.

play   stay   rain   paint

Then Grandma groaned from inside the wardrobe.

The woodcutter grabbed the handle and let Grandma out.

Sound out some words that begin with the gr blend.

grip   gravy   growl   greedy

grill   group   grass

"Thank you!" said Grandma, grinning at the woodcutter, and grabbing Red Riding Hood for a great big hug.

Stick on speech bubbles for each person.

Well done!

Use your stickers to **spell** more words beginning with the gr blend.

grid   grow   green   grand

Sound out these words, which all use the k sound made by c and k.

cut   cow   card   castle

kiss   key   kitten

"This is cause for cake and a cup of coffee!" said Grandma, and went into the kitchen to put the kettle on, and fetch some cupcakes.

Well done!

Say the words as you spot things beginning with the **k** sound.

Stick on their stickers.

cake stand

cupcake

cup

21

The wolf had had **quite** enough for one day. He went to live a **quiet** life deep in the wood and **quivered** and **quaked** whenever he saw Red Riding Hood!

Use your stickers to **spell** some words beginning with qu.

quite   qu**een**   qu**ilt**   qu**ick**

Ask your child to **retell** the story using these key sounds and story images.

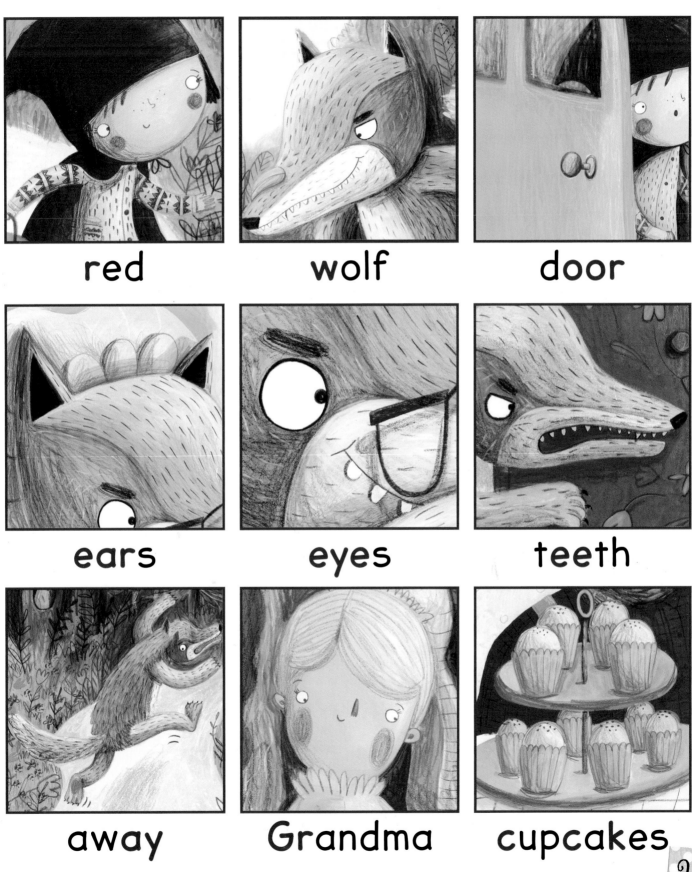

red

wolf

door

ears

eyes

teeth

away

Grandma

cupcakes

Use your stickers to **add** a word that matches
the red highlighted **sounds** on each line.

good   could   foot   [ ]

usual   casual   leisure

knew   nightcap   knock

saw   autumn   door

eye   high   fly

feet   treat   bead

face   life   wolf

his   hedge   have

quick   queen   quit

You've had fun with phonics! Well done.